GUINNESS

SELF DEFENCE

The Complete Course

A simple, practical step-by-step guide for all

JOHN GOLDMAN 4TH DAN BLACK BELT BUJITSU (SELF DEFENCE)

First published in 1988 by Guinness Publishing Limited, 33 London Road, Enfield, Middlesex EN2 6DJ.

Created, designed and produced by Facer Publishing Limited, 7 Colleton Crescent, Exeter, Devon EX2 4DG, England.

British Library Cataloguing in Publication Data
Goldman, John
 Self defence.
 1. Self-defence – Manuals
 I. Title
 613.6'6

 ISBN 0-85112-331-7

***Guinness* is a registered trademark of Guinness Superlatives Limited.**

Photography by Charles Willis with additional photographs by Terry Matthews.
Edited by Rob Kendrew.
Design by Laurence Daeche.

Typesetting by P&M Typesetting Limited, Exeter, England.
Mono and colour origination by Peninsular Repro Service Limited, Exeter, England.
Printed and bound in Great Britain by Purnell Book Production Limited, Paulton, Bristol.

The publishers wish to thank the following people for the their help and assistance in the preparation of this book: Stephanie Chaplin, Simon Milward, Peter Scully (General Manager, *The Plaza*, Exeter).

CONTENTS

THE AUTHOR

John Goldman is a full-time professional teacher of self defence and Judo. He holds the rank of Black Belt 4th Dan in both these arts and is an instructor for the largest independent martial arts association in the United Kingdom – the Amateur Martial Association. He is also the author of *Judo The Complete Course* (Guinness Books 1986).

John has many different kinds of pupil from the very young to civilian adults and police. He also takes a special class of deaf children.

In 1982 he visited Japan as a guest of the world-renowned Judo master, the late Abbe Sensei. Abbe Sensei awarded John his 4th Dan Judo and became the acknowledged Master of the Universal Budo Association of which John is Secretary and a founder member.

John's first training was in Judo. Whilst specialising in Judo he realised that a comprehensive defence system required more than his Judo skills. He looked closely at the arts of Aikido and Karate and their approaches to defence. One thing John insists on is that there must be a difference in attitude between training for a sport and becoming equipped to face real-life situations. The essence of John's approach to self defence is that it MUST WORK.

DEDICATION

To my daughters Ruth and Jenny

FOREWORD

The martial arts in Japan have never lost the essential element of self defence in which they had their origin. In a world in which attacks on the person have increased, the martial arts can be of service to the modern forms of self defence.

John Goldman is fully aware of the contribution the martial arts make to self defence. His special skill, demonstrated in this book, lies in adapting their techniques to the practical needs of society.

Self Defence – The Complete Course marks a new and important step forward in the practice of self defence.

Mitsunori Sato
Professor of Judo

Mr Sato, professor of Judo, is a leading European figurehead of the martial arts. He left the Nippon University, Japan to take the post of Chief Instructor to the Danish Police Force. He now resides in Majorca, Spain, where he has established his European martial arts centre 'Shubukan'. Professor Sato, personal friend to the author, travels Europe giving seminars. His technical brilliance has been much appreciated by those who have attended his courses in England.

INTRODUCTION

Here at last is a clearly illustrated step-by-step guide to self defence for all. The pictures and explanations are specially arranged to show how the techniques work. Many can be practised safely and easily in a limited space.

Although it is recognised that women are particularly vulnerable to attack, young people and older alike, of both sexes, are faced with dangers. So whether you are a beginner or are a more experienced member of a self defence or martial art class, this manual will serve as an invaluable companion and reference.

WHY DO I NEED TO DEFEND MYSELF?

Attacks on people are the history of mankind. In more recent times, footpads and highwaymen have given place to muggers. A later development is the spread of violence to nurses in hospitals and social service workers on their rounds. People in both professions are seeking ways of protecting themselves. Even the managements of chain stores are becoming concerned about their staff, encouraging their employees to train in self defence.

The police can only do so much. It is becoming wise for people in many walks of life, and for lonely householders too, to equip themselves to deal with at least some forms of attack. Look, for instance, at a situation which is becoming only too tragically familiar. A woman, walking alone, is waylaid by a man. He will first weigh up his chances, then pursue his advantages stage-by-stage to the point where she is mercilessly raped.

The very earliest point of confrontation could be vital. He may have the choice of a dozen different ways of making his attack. If he finds, to his pain and astonishment, that his would-be victim is ready for him, whichever way he moves, he is a potential loser.

People need not be helpless in the face of attack. The key to self-protection is preparation. Training for self defence calls to its aid the long history of the martial arts. Nevertheless, self defence in its modern form is a separate skill. It can be taught. Your limbs and your body are superb tools; now you need to learn how to use them as weapons – for your defence.

You may never require them to function in this way, but how much better for you to know that you could use them if you had to.

WILL I BE ABLE TO DEFEND MYSELF?

The answer is YES
— *if* you are prepared to look at self defence realistically, and
— *if* you learn to ● reduce the risks
　　　　　　　● achieve certain skills which can be taught.

This book demonstrates defensive action that is within the capacity of everybody. Anyone can, for instance, take initial precautions against attack such as are shown on pages 10–13 or if they *are* attacked, meet it with such a simple action as bending the aggressor's finger.

Many of the techniques demonstrated in this book can be practised safely at home or, if facilities are provided, at your place of work.

For a full mastery of all the techniques available you should practise under expert tuition. Ineffective training is dangerous and can lead to a false sense of security. It is like a faulty fire extinguisher that could give a feeling of confidence for 20 years and be found tragically wanting when the fire breaks out. There is no doubt that with proper training most people *can* gain the initiative in an attack, either by frightening away or disabling the attacker. Training in self defence will take a person to a point just short of inflicting real injury. It sounds brutal. It is brutal.

Unwelcome attentions? A glass of squash may be enough to cool him off.

FACT AND FANTASY

"What is spectacular is not always practical. What is practical is not always spectacular".

This was said by the late Bruce Lee, who was known world-wide for his martial arts films in the early 1970s.

What we see in the movies is complete fantasy – the hero always wins and his opponent always loses because it is his job to lose. Punches are thrown on the screen that would cause serious injury in real life and yet the hero emerges unscathed after a rain of blows. Screen fights are staged between professional stuntmen who know how to fight and how to make a fight *look* good.

To defend yourself effectively you must rid your mind of all these images and deal only in realities. I am sometimes asked by students at self defence classes "Can I protect myself if I am attacked by a number of people at the same time?"

You are obviously better off with training in self defence than having no training at all. But heavily superior odds will almost certainly win the day unless, of course, the attackers' surprise at finding themselves faced with skilled resistance frightens them off. People are much more likely, however, to be attacked by a single aggressor than by a group.

SELF DEFENCE & THE MARTIAL ARTS

Self defence has grown out of the traditional martial arts like Judo and Karate and is increasingly being taught as a separate skill.

In the traditional martial arts, attack is often concentrated on certain parts of the body. This is a throwback from the past when warriors wore armour and blows were aimed at the weak points and joints in the armour. Today's martial arts are still taught with this underlying idea. They are also governed by acknowledged rules of combat. In the real world, bag-snatchers or rapists do not wear armour or follow any rules.

In self defence it is not enough to know what you would do in certain limited circumstances – that is the basis of the martial arts. Self defence is all systems go. It is a massive irresistible explosion but a controlled one as a result of careful training. You must not lose your temper but find your temper.

Training in the martial arts still offers many advantages for self defence. It will give you more confidence, make you more alert, fitter and better equipped with certain fundamental skills. These skills are a help but it must be emphasised that, unlike the martial arts, self defence is not for belts but for survival.

SELF DEFENCE & THE LAW

The law is not always clear on what you may or may not do in your own defence (often this is decided in the courts) but here are some guidelines.

- If you are attacked, you have every right to defend yourself but you may only use as much force as is reasonably necessary to ward off an attacker.

- Everyday items which you might normally be expected to carry – an umbrella, a walking stick, car keys etc – may be used against an attacker.

The law does not allow you to carry anything which can be described as an offensive weapon. This rules out articles *designed* to cause injury, such as knuckledusters. You may not carry an article *adapted* to cause injury, such as a sharpened comb. A cricket bat is an offensive weapon if it is taken out with the *intention* of using it to inflict injury. Similarly, if you went out with an umbrella with the *intention* of hitting somebody with it, the umbrella becomes an offensive weapon. Stones can be offensive weapons but if you were attacked and found yourself lying in the ground with a stone to hand, it would be reasonable to use it against your attacker.

Once attacked, you have to decide immediately how to defend yourself. This may mean inflicting pain on your attacker – jabbing with the point of an umbrella or a bunch of keys. You can't afford to be squeamish about this. You do what is necessary to stop the attack.

Chris is followed. She phones for help.

The man bursts into the telephone box.

Chris uses the phone as a weapon. Her quick thinking should help her escape.

REDUCING THE RISKS

PRECAUTIONS IN THE STREET

How safe are we in the street?

The unexpected can always happen during the day as well as at night. But attacks are more likely if they are invited. The woman who dresses up and goes out on her own at night and chooses lonely ill-lit streets is taking an unnecessary risk (whether she realises it or not).

Shoppers can be seen in any supermarket with trolleys full to the brim and a handbag thrown carelessly on top.

These are just two situations which clearly spell danger.

There are many simple ways of reducing risks – for men or women, young or old:

- Choose your route. Well-used streets are safest.
- Don't take short cuts through dimly lit areas.
- Must you be alone? Is there anyone who can accompany you?
- Face oncoming traffic. It is easier to escape the unwelcome attentions from the driver of a car pointed in the opposite direction.
- Don't hitch hike. If you miss the last bus or train, a taxi is worth the expense.
- Your appearance is important. Wear a coat over a party dress.
- Walk with confident steps. Don't look nervous. Try and keep calm – breathe deeply.
- Don't walk close to hedges and dark doorways.
- Carry only what you need. Separate your cheque book and cheque cards. Don't take more money than you need.
- Don't carry your wallet in your back pocket. The safest pocket for money (including notes) is the left-hand trouser pocket.
- For women shoulder bags are best. Hold these close to your body with the flaps innermost.
- Don't put your purse on top of the shopping or in any other visible place.
- Have your house or car keys ready in your hand so you can open the door and get in quickly.
- Avoid empty carriages in trains and the top decks of buses.

There are many kinds of hand-held alarms that can be used in the street or in the home. But remember to keep them accessible for immediate use.

REDUCING THE RISKS

PRECAUTIONS IN THE HOME

Violence is on the increase but attacks in the home are still comparatively rare. Four out of every five burglaries take place during the daytime when the house is empty. A mounting number of milk bottles on the doorstep and a pile of newspapers and daily post are clear signs that a house is unoccupied. Cancelling the milk and newspapers and having a neighbour collect the mail will help to reduce these risks.

A break-in at an occupied house can of course be dangerous for the occupant and sometimes even fatal. There are many simple precautions that you can take to protect your home:

- House door plates should have initials only before your surname. Omit "Miss" or "Mrs". Enter your name similarly in directories.
- Fit an outside porchlight. There are several types: those you switch on; those with a time switch; others light automatically as a visitor approaches.
- Always use a door-chain. It is useful to fit a viewer to inspect visitors.
- Security locks and bolts for all doors and windows are easily fitted.
- Before you leave your house, shut all doors and windows. Even if you are only going next door, close your own door.
- Draw your curtains at night.
- If you go out, leave one or two room lights on and also a radio.
- Let your baby-sitter know where you are going. Leave a telephone number.

These are just some of the precautions you can take. The police are always willing to give advice on security.

There is always danger in allowing strangers into your home. Bogus officials or so-called "dealers" and "workmen", once over the doorstep, can be menacing and even violent. The elderly are particularly vulnerable.

What should you do when someone comes to your door?

- The chain should always be in place. Do not take it off until you are sure of the identity of your caller.
- It is your home, you are hospitable and your first instinct is to trust the caller. It is important however that you drill yourself to overcome the instinct to throw open the door and even invite them into your home.

Even a person (and it could be a woman) claiming to represent a well-known charity could be bogus. You are *not* silly to keep a barrier between you and them until you are absolutely certain that they are genuine.

- Ask for proof of identity. Check this carefully.
- Telephone their organisation for confirmation that they are a genuine representative.
- An official should have your account number (have this ready for checking).
- If you are at all suspicious, telephone the police.

Remember the bogus caller is often a professional. *Do not allow him to pressurise you.*

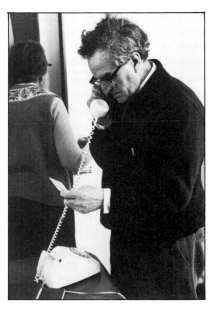

WEAPONS OF THE BODY

You are now aware that you can reduce risks by taking sensible precautions. You have the equipment in your own physical make-up to protect yourself. Your body is a weapon or a variety of weapons. What you need is first, commitment and second the mastery of techniques which offer you a full defence system.

The way you react to any situation depends on your own personality as well as the skills learned from this book. For instance, you may be able to use a shout or a scream to good purpose but think yourself incapable of poking someone in the eye. At the end of the day you must exercise your right to defend yourself and overcome a natural revulsion to some kinds of action.

The shouting of the word "NO!" or even swearing is a defence technique. Screaming will often be as much a deterrent to an attacker as any number of defence moves. Running away is also a technique but more positive action may be needed. A hand flicked to an attacker's face, a kick, a dig with the elbow may be enough to distract him from his purpose, whatever that may be.

Distracting the aggressor could, with good timing, be the most important of your techniques. Prompt action may frighten away an attacker or provide you with a chance to escape, but you can't count on it. You must learn follow-up moves. Once you have mastered a number of techniques, with the help of this book, you can pursue your aggressive defence to the point where you are free, or even to the disablement of your attacker.

Consider these two words:

   **MOVEMENT ▶ ▶ ▶**

Your explosion must be immediate, violent and controlled. Control comes from knowing how to use your body and the weapons it provides you with. Movement involves the total use of your whole body as an effective response to attack, and again this comes with training.

Explosion and movement are not separate. They combine into a force which few people realise they possess. In the end you have to decide what you will *actually* do. There may well be a time when *any* action on your part could endanger your life. If your choice is for action, this book is a guide to the best use of your natural ability to defend yourself.

People think of weapons as objects to be wielded but, in fact, the human body is in many ways equipped with "weapons". All you need is the skill, knowledge and determination which enable you to make effective use of many parts of your body in your own defence.

There are varying degrees of severity with which you make use of these means. For instance, if a man puts his arm around a woman in a pub, she may only need to push him away with the open palm of her hand. However, if she were being annoyed in a lonely park she would clearly have to employ a more drastic response – perhaps applying the same open palm with some force to his nose.

Think first about using your hands. Look at the different striking positions open to you.

USING YOUR HANDS

The heel of your palm

The side of your hand

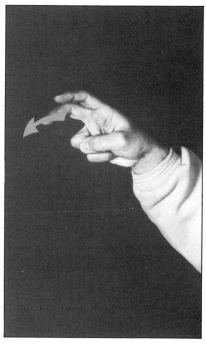

Your clawing fingers

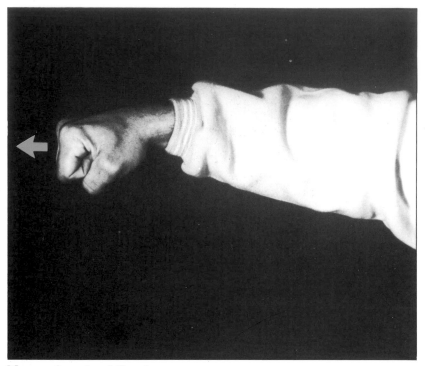

Your clenched fist (a clenched fist should always have the thumb on the outside)

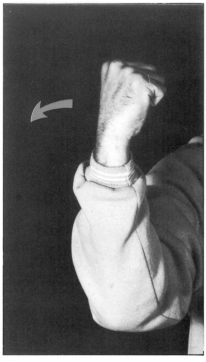

The back of your fist

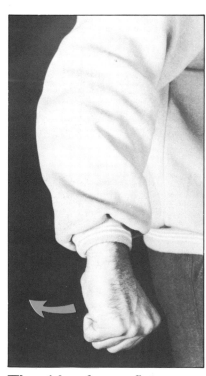

The side of your fist

Your extended knuckle

USING THE REST OF YOUR BODY

Other parts of the body can also become striking weapons.

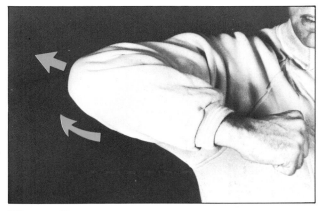

Your elbow

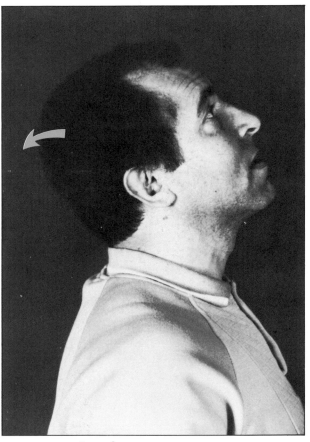

Even your head ...

Your foot

Your knee

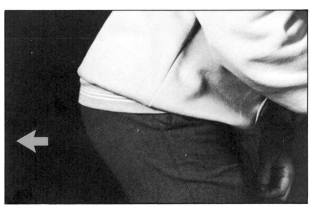

... and backside.

DISTRACTION TECHNIQUES

If you are attacked you are at an immediate disadvantage. The aggressor has a plan, but you are taken by surprise. You need to act swiftly to upset his plan by distracting him. You have a number of means of doing this.

Distraction may be enough to put him off or stop him completely. You will be most effective if you overcome any squeamishness about what you do. If you are prepared to push, poke, pinch and pound you are now in a position to counter-attack.

STRIKES

Chris strikes for the face.

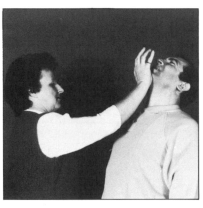

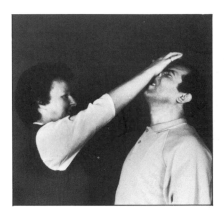

With the palm of her hand, she strikes her assailant on the chin ...

... or to the nose.

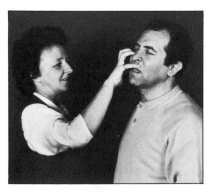

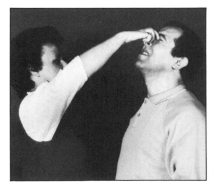

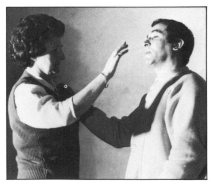

Clawing at the face is usually both unexpected and effective ...

... particularly if it is aimed at the attacker's eyes.

A hand flashed quickly across the attacker's eyes without necessarily making contact will distract him and put him off his stride.

Twisting and pinching loose and sensitive areas of flesh will often distract the attacker enough to put him off his guard.

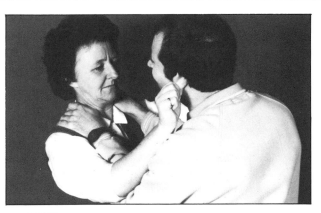

Chris pinches sensitive areas ...

... ears ...

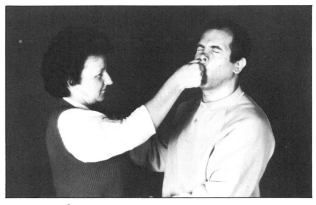

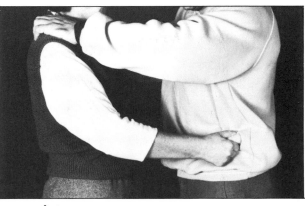

... mouth or ...

... waist.

Distraction techniques may often be enough to break an attacker's hold on you.

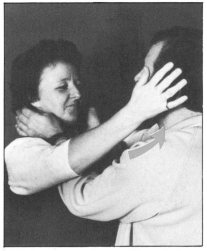

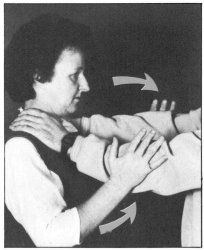

With the palms of both her hands Chris slams hard against her attacker's ears...

... or his elbow joints.

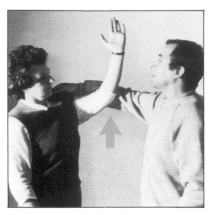

Chris breaks the attacker's grip by thrusting up her arms.

Either one single arm ...

... or both of them.

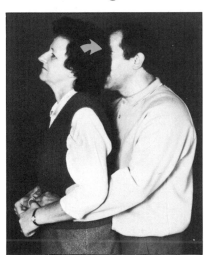

Here Chris is attacked from behind. Back goes her head, or up goes her elbow – into her attacker's face.

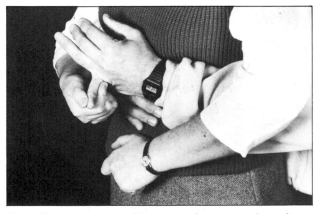

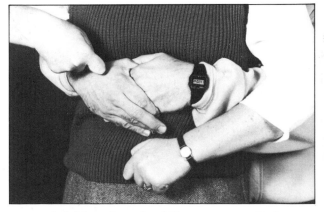

Another way to distract the attacker is by bending back a finger...

... or jabbing hard with an extended knuckle on the sensitive area at the back of the hand. Try this on your own hand: it's painful!

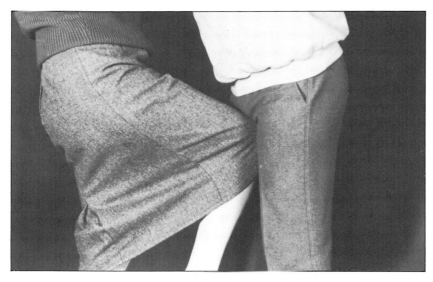

KICKS

An unexpected kick can be one of the most effective of distraction techniques.

A knee in the groin is often effective. However, it might not be the complete answer. Follow-on techniques after using your knee are shown later.

Three kinds of kick:

Back kick to the groin – if you are attacked from behind.

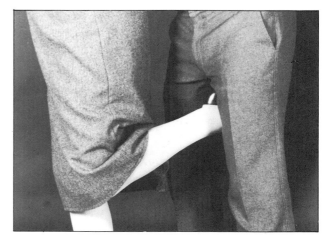

Back and front kicks to the sensitive knee joint.

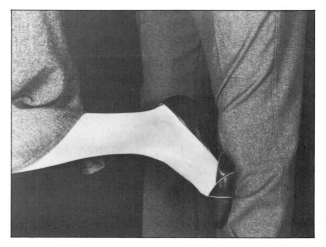

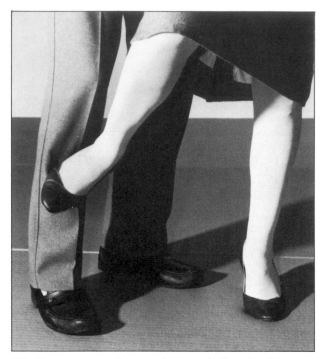

Chris scrapes down the attacker's shin with the hard sole of her shoe ...

... or stamps with her heel hard onto her attacker's foot.

Distraction is the start of your defence. You will find many of the above distraction techniques repeated in later sections of the book, shown in real-life situations. Many of them can be combined into an explosive counter-attack which in itself could be enough to stop an aggressor.

HOW TO USE YOUR STRENGTH

When a woman is attacked by a man she is almost certainly the weaker. What training in self defence does is vastly increase the effectiveness of her limited physical strength by applying it where it counts. This is often true for men as well as women.

Try the following:

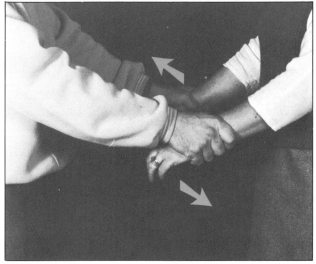

Get a friend to grab you by your wrists. Try to force his hands apart. Difficult?

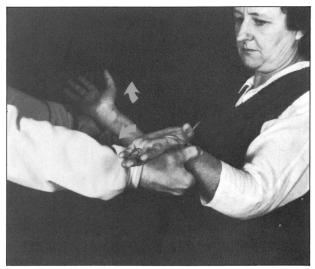

Open your hands quickly outwards. His grip is broken.

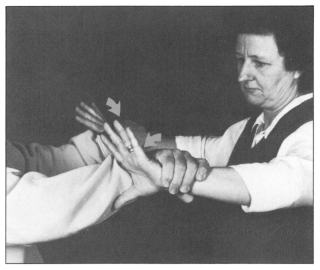

Let him re-apply his grip. This time turn your hands up and inwards. Not only does this break his grip but by pushing down

with your hands you can cause considerable pain to his wrists. (See the later section on arm locking, pages 26-29)

HOW TO USE YOUR STRENGTH

Your friend takes you by the wrist. Try to pull yourself free. Problems?

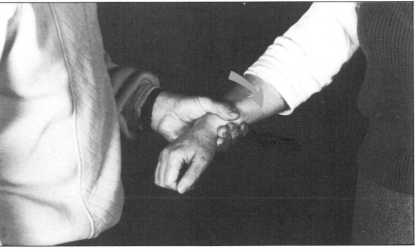

Now twist your hand sharply so that the thinner side of your wrist is between his fingers and thumb.

Problem solved. You can pull free much more easily.

This time your partner grasps your wrist with two hands. How do you break out of this one?

Reach through and take hold of your own hand.

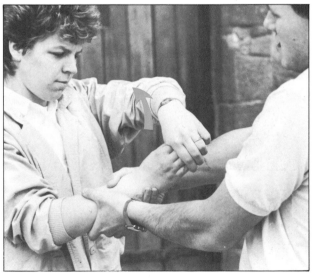

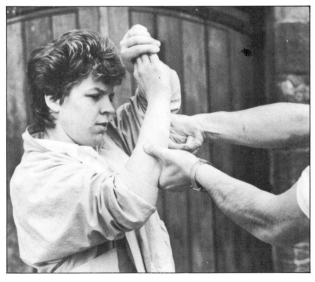

Pull sharply upwards ...

... you're free.

Practise these moves with a friend until you can perform them naturally and spontaneously.

LOCKING

ARM LOCKING

A lock is the application of pressure against a joint forcing it into an unnatural position. This will cause pain. Excessive pressure can cause torn muscles and ligaments and broken bones.

It is important to remember that when you practise these potentially dangerous moves you must be careful not to exert too much pressure. If you go to a self defence class you will be taken through warming up exercises. If you practise at home make sure you warm up your joints by swinging your arms, rotating wrists or doing press-ups – in fact any moves which ensure that your joints are more flexible.

The following pictures show locks to different parts of the arm.

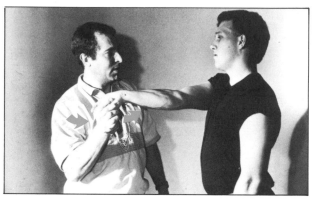

The hand is held palm upwards. It is now a simple matter to push him backwards, forcing his hand painfully against his wrist joint.

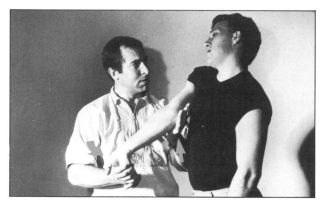

I follow this through by pushing my hand under his elbow joint. There are now counter-pressures and great strain on his elbow.

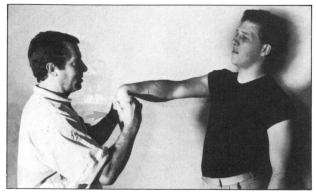

I place both my thumbs on the back of his wrist and push.

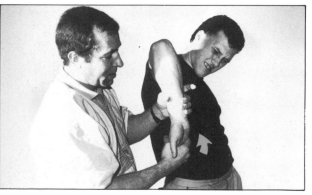

Holding his wrist in my left hand, I grip his fingers with my right hand and twist anti-clockwise.

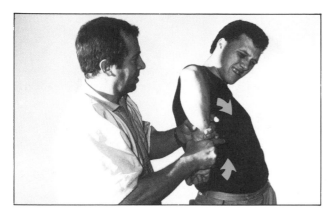

There is a double twist here. Both my hands are on his wrist, my right hand turning inwards and my left hand outwards.

Throughout the book you will see that the would-be victim often turns the tables on her attacker and applies the following simple wrist-lock.

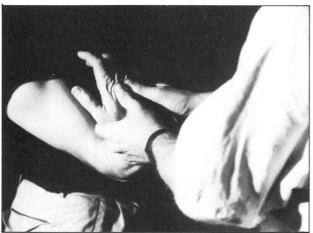

With my thumbs on the back of his hand...

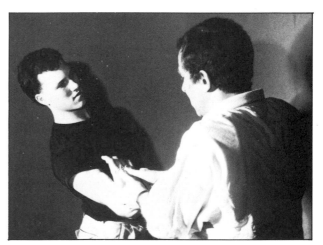

... I force back his wrist.

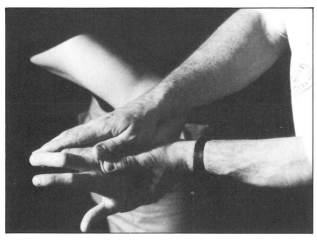

There is additional touch to this hold. I turn his hand sideways, pressing down with the palm of my right hand.

Note that I still maintain the pressure to the back of his hand with my left thumb.

If you have your attacker on the ground, this may well be the time to make yourself scarce. However, the following pictures show how an assailant can be further restrained.

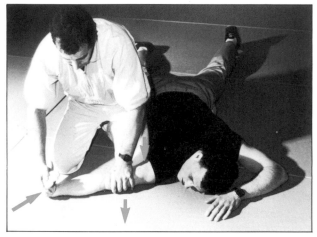

My left hand and knee keep his arm firmly on the ground. With my right hand I bend his wrist.

I have changed the position of his arm but the lock is just as effective.

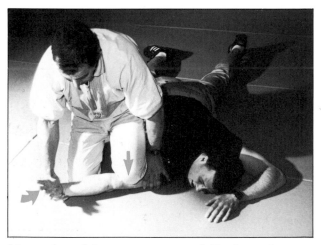

I kneel on his upper arm while levering up his lower arm. This counter-movement puts a terrific strain on his elbow joint.

Note also the counter-pressure in this picture.

Once you have taken hold of your attacker's palm and wrist there are other directions you can move in. Try them!

Here again another lock depends for its effectiveness on counter-pressures.

Ouch! A real tangle.

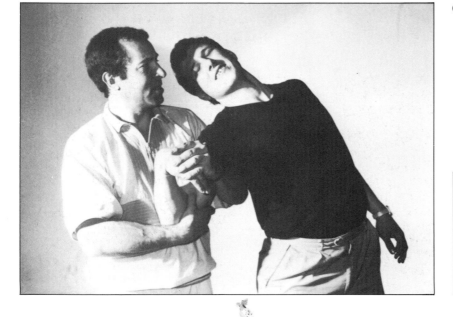

In later sections of the book you will see many of the techniques already described demonstrated in real life situations as part of other moves.

LEG LOCKING

Your legs too are useful for applying locks. You could be on the ground with your attacker standing over you.

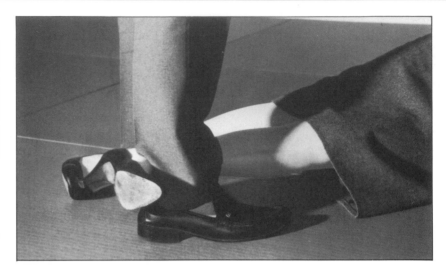

One lock to apply in this situation is to hook one leg around his ankle.

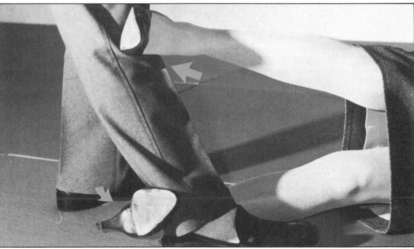

... and holding this firmly, crack hard into his knee with your other foot.

This locks the knee, inflicts severe pain and will make it very difficult for your attacker to maintain his balance.

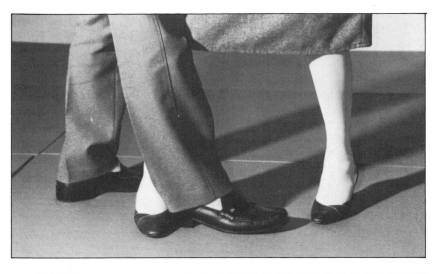

You and your assailant may both be standing however.

Here Chris hooks her leg firmly behind my ankle and ...

... presses her knee against mine, locking the joint. Now all she has to do is push with her arms and ...

... over I go.

TRIPPING

By applying the techniques described above you may have weakened the attacker. Tripping him up may now be enough to allow you to escape.

The simplest trip is where your foot goes outside and behind his leg. All you need do then is push him over and run.

This time, keeping your weight on your left leg, you lift your right leg back and up, forcing up his leg. This unbalances him. A push finishes the job.

This picture shows how the technique can work in practice.

Here your foot goes inside and behind his leg. For this technique keep your foot firmly planted on the floor. You can then push him over.

Or, by bending your knee and lifting your leg you can topple him.

And, again in a real life situation, Ruth shows how this technique works out.

So far we have been talking in theoretical terms. Now we enter the realm of grim reality. The rest of the book deals with the way you meet many forms of attack – grabbing, attempted strangulation, hair pulling or other kinds of assault.

As you follow these attacks and ways of dealing with them, you will see that techniques already demonstrated (such as distraction, locking and tripping) keep coming up again. Refer back to the earlier pages to check detail.

Ruth is grabbed by her attacker in a bear-hug. Her arms are still free however.

To distract him she instantly claws at his face or ...

... twists his ear.

This could be enough to deter the assailant, particularly if there are other people about. The essential thing about even the most basic response to attack, is that it is *immediate* and *forceful* – an almost instinctive response. This spontaneity can only result from a lot of practice either at home or in a class.

Chris applies three distraction techniques simultaneously when she is grabbed from the front and pushed against a fence.

She pinches the sensitive area around his waist, pushes his body away from her and at the same time stamps her foot down into the back of his knee.

Or she jabs her pointed knuckle into his neck and crashes her knee up into his groin.

As Ruth is attacked from the front she thrusts her own knees forward into his. This locks his knee joints and gives her the required space between them either to ...

... shove her knee into his groin or ...

... by stepping between his legs ...

... and pushing ...

... to send him crashing to the ground. Her main object now is to get away quickly, even if it means leaving her handbag on the ground.

HELD FROM BEHIND

Ruth is attacked from behind. Her arms are still free.

She immediately turns and strikes back at his head with her elbow ...

... or, if her arms *were* pinned, she could jerk her head hard back into his face.

She can at the same time scrape her foot down his shin or ...

... stamp her heel onto his foot. Imagine the pain this would cause if you were wearing pointed heels!

This attack comes from behind.

Ruth immediately throws back her hips into his stomach upsetting his balance.

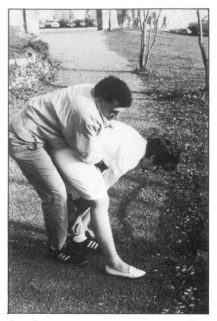

In the same movement she reaches down between her legs and seizes his ankle.

A vigorous pull upwards ...

... and he's grounded. Ruth completes the job by kicking back into his groin before making a get-away.

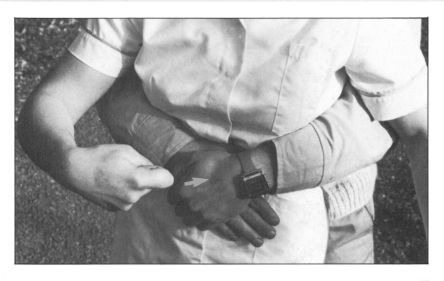

Another way: striking the back of his hand with an extended knuckle ...

... Ruth breaks his grip. This distraction technique could be enough to enable her to get away.

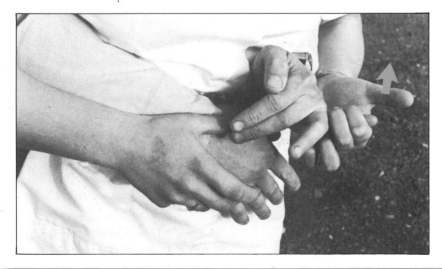

Alternatively she could wrench back his little finger.

The next technique needs special practice. It is not difficult for most people but should be rehearsed in club conditions under expert instruction.

Ruth is grabbed from behind. Her arms are pinned. She distracts her attacker and weakens his grip by kicking back into his shin with her heel.

She drops down onto one knee, takes hold of the sleeve of his jacket and pulls hard.

She bends forward, still tugging at his sleeve and she throws him over her shoulder.

He falls. She could now apply an arm lock (as seen earlier on pages 26–29) to prevent her attacker from regaining his feet or she could make a quick retreat.

Another simple distraction would have been for Ruth to stamp forcefully on his foot.

In this attack Ruth's arms were pinned by her assailant, which changed her response. Since she could not use her arms for distraction, she used her feet. Ruth could just as easily thrust her head back into his face.

HELD BY THE WRISTS

These techniques demonstrate how to turn your strength, even if it is limited, into explosive movement. You will recognise techniques we have already demonstrated in the studio. They are now brought together in a real situation. You now see how devastating they are.

Ruth is held by both wrists.

She flings her arms upwards and outwards (this breaks his grip) ...

... and kicks his shin.

Again Ruth is subjected to a wrist hold.

This time as her arms go up she twists them inwards so that the palms of her hands turn outwards.

By pressing downwards she locks his wrists (see page 23).

Ruth's knees could now inflict damage if necessary.

Ruth responds to her attacker's double wrist hold by . . .

. . . flinging one arm up and one arm outwards. At the same time she steps forward.

Her leg goes behind his to trip him.

He falls to the ground, giving her a chance to get away.

Remember — from the word go, in self defence continuous action is everything. Hesitation invites disaster.

As Ruth is grabbed by the wrist ...

... she twists her arm, bringing the thinner part of her wrist between his fingers and thumb and she ...

... sharply pulls away.

You must be prepared for an attacker using either hand and be ready with both hands.

Here he reaches for Ruth's wrist with his right hand.

In one swift movement she pulls her arm back and upwards.

This loosens his grip and enables Ruth to thrust forward with her forearm.

This positions her elbow above his chest ...

... and down she comes with it with all the power of her body behind her.

It all starts again from a wrist hold.

Ruth flings her arm outwards, opening her hand. This movement pulls his arm into an unnatural position.

Ruth brings up her free arm to grip her attacker just above the elbow joint.

She turns her whole body ...

... pushing down on his elbow joint, while keeping a grip on his wrist.

He can't save himself!
Ruth can get away or ...

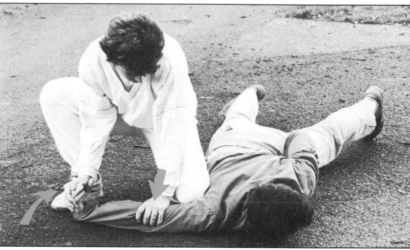

... put an arm lock on him.

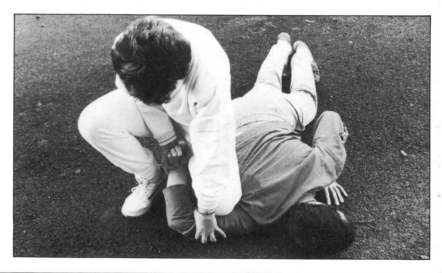

As the attacker takes hold of Ruth's wrist she immediately clamps her other hand on top of his with her thumb underneath – she wants to keep him there.

Ruth turns her hand upwards and outwards. This rotation brings her hand on top of his wrist. She must keep his hand in this twisted position.

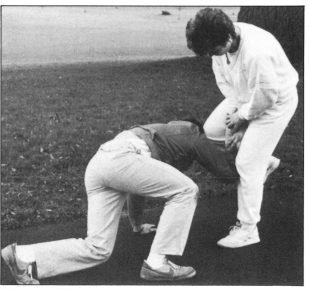

She could now continue to draw him forward and hit him in the head with her knee.

She pulls down with her arms. The pain forces her attacker to his knees.

My attacker holds my wrists from behind.

I move to one side and throw one arm up and one out, stepping back under his right arm.

This brings me to his side. This movement weakens his grip on both my arms. I am now able with my left hand to grip his right wrist. His right arm, as you see, is twisted.

To keep control over him I bring my right hand into play (this lock is shown in more detail on page 26).

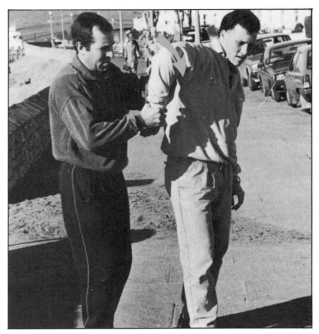

This might be enough but I could ...

... steer him to the ground by forcing down his right arm at the elbow joint.

Another way to escape from a hold from behind: as I turn under, and the attacker's grip is weakened ...

... I take hold of his wrists.

I am now in control, tying him into a knot with one of his arms locking the other at the elbow.

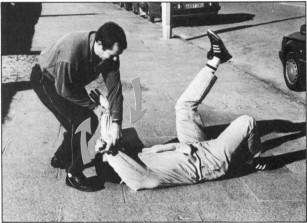

One swift turn and he's over.

A simple technique. I respond to his grip on my wrist by ...

... raising my foot ...

... and stamping into his knee.

There are two important points to note here. One is that this kind of kick has great force. The other is that a person on the attack is putting full weight onto his legs. This gives him little flexibility and something is likely to go – probably his knee-cap.

In earlier techniques Ruth's hand was turned with the palm downwards. In this wrist hold it is turned upwards. Her response must therefore be different.

She pulls him towards her, turning her hand to ...

... grip his wrist.

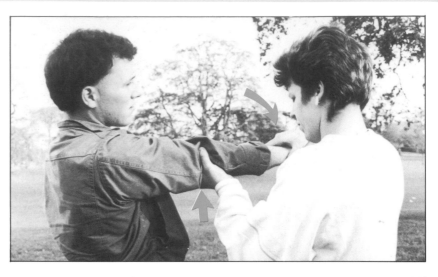

With her free left hand she strikes upwards forcing his elbow back.

She keeps pulling forward, at the same time ...

... taking his arm over her shoulder ...

... and forcing it violently down against his elbow joint.

This shows the same move from the front. Ruth has now extended her left leg. She continues to pull ...

... and there is nowhere to go but down.

Follow this through slowly; it's not as difficult as it looks.

Ruth's wrist is gripped once more.

She pulls her attacker towards her, raising her arm so that she can step underneath and she ...

... turns.

This has twisted his arm back on itself.

Stepping forward, she
pulls down on his wrist
with her right hand and
with her left pushes down
on his elbow.

The inevitable end.

HELD BY THE HAIR

Your hair is a vulnerable part of your body and an obvious target for any attacker. An attacker is not deterred by the pain he may cause you. If your hair is pulled, never resist by backing away; this only increases the pain. Your first move must be to take off the pressure.

FROM THE FRONT

Ruth is grabbed by the hair. She immediately lets go of her bag which he is after and ...

... clamps her hands tight over his. This must be an instant reaction.

While she keeps her grip on his hand – in effect making it part of her head – she moves backwards and lowers her head.

Note how the attacker's wrist is bent backwards. It is now he who is feeling the pain.

Ruth keeps stepping backwards until ...

... he's flat on the ground. Ruth can now run away. In this instance she has kept hold of her bag. The important thing though is to get away, even if this means leaving the bag behind.

Another way: once Ruth has secured his hand to her head ...

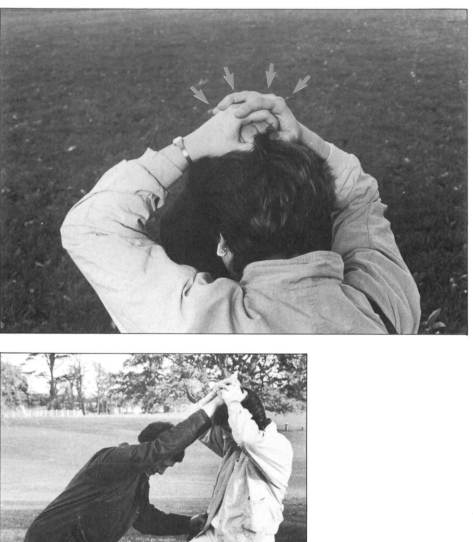

... she can simply kick his shin. This might be enough for him to release his grip.

This time Ruth clamps one of her hands to the back of his – her other hand clasps his wrist.

Ruth then turns round smartly and...

... with the help of her elbow puts on a painful lock.

HELD BY THE HAIR

HAIR PULLED FROM BEHIND

As **Ruth's** attacker grabs her hair from behind she takes off the pressure by clamping his hand with hers and ...

... spinning round towards him ...

... she slams the back of her fist into his face. This is a very powerful strike (see page 16).

This time as her attacker grabs her hair from behind ...

... Ruth spins round and swings one fist back into his groin.

Another way: Ruth strikes back with her leg to his shin or up into the groin.

This hair pull defence finishes with Ruth putting a wrist lock on her attacker.

As she clamps his hand to her head ...

... she turns and ducks under his arm.

When she comes up...

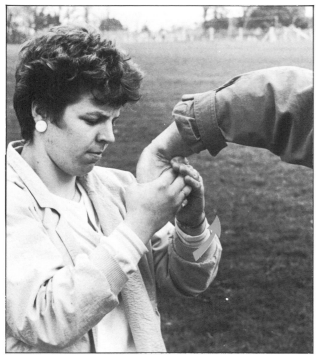

...she has put on a painful wrist lock.

Ruth can follow this through with a strike ...

... to his elbow ...

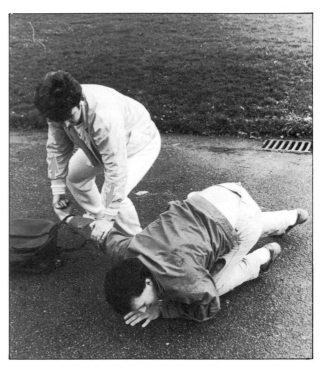

... forcing him to the ground.

The following sequences have been staged in studio conditions so that the power and speed of using your body to the full can be better demonstrated. Note that in two of the sequences I end up on the ground with my attacker. It is not a good idea to go down with your attacker unless you do so while still maintaining full control of the situation. In the following pictures you will see that I have exercised enough force, while keeping control, to ensure that my attacker is no longer able to return to the conflict.

As Nigel takes hold of my lapel I strike to his face. This is essentially to distract him. If you make contact it can cause severe injury. So much the worse for the attacker!

I follow through with my right hand. I have now taken hold of his hand with my thumb on top (you saw this grip on page 27).

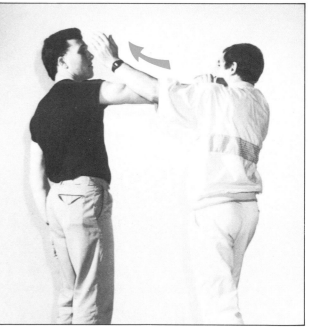

I turn in towards him, still keeping hold of his hand, and swing my left arm up ...

... and over his arm. This twists his arm.

... I drop down, using the weight of my body against his shoulder. This slams him flat on his face. Note that his right arm is now in a powerful lock.

My lapel is held. I strike for Nigel's eyes.

As in the last technique, I take his hand with my thumb hard on the back.

As I twist his arm in an attempt to bring him to the ground ...

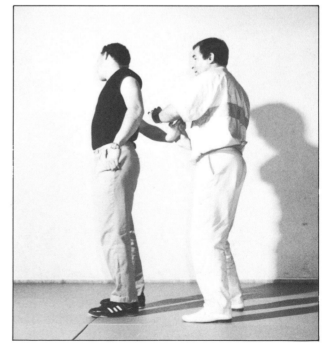

... he too turns to take off the pressure.

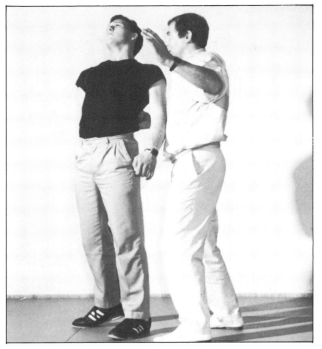

I respond by slapping my open left hand to his throat.

As you can see from the front, this throws him off balance.

I continue to push until he falls to the ground. He is in a nasty mess with his right arm stuck behind his back.

Nigel grips my lapels with both hands

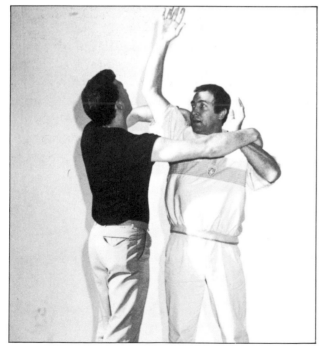

I throw my right arm up in the air between his arms. This is sudden and forceful – explosive. I may hit his face on the way up. This has broken his hold.

My right arm bears down on the back of his neck, forcing down his head.

This enables me to lock his head against my body.

This shot from a different angle shows how I control his head. The technique calls for great care if you are practising with friends; it puts tremendous pressure on the neck.

When Nigel takes hold of my lapel, I grasp his wrist, at the same time striking to his face. As his grip weakens ...

... I pull his arm across my chest. At the same time my right arm stretches across his body ...

... forcing him to the ground. Note that his left arm is braced across my chest locking his elbow.

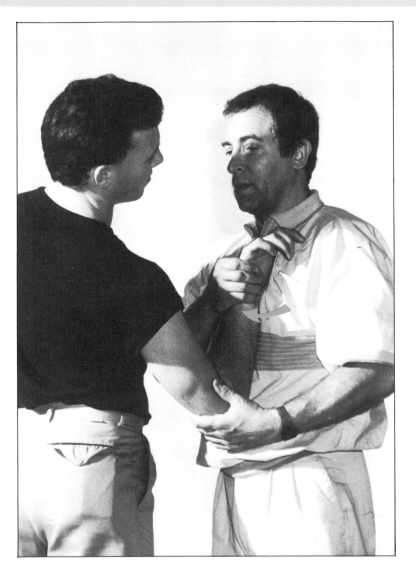

In this move, **Nigel's** lapel hold has been broken by my grasping and twisting his right wrist with my fingers on his palm and my thumb on the back of his hand. With my other hand I stop his elbow from moving. This is a technique of its own and may be enough to deter him.

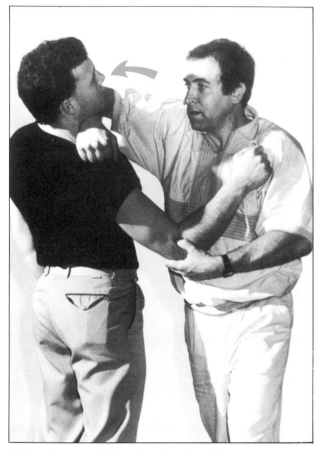

This time as **N**igel takes hold, I weaken his right arm by pressing my thumb into the pressure point near his elbow. With my right forearm I strike into his throat and grip his right shoulder.

I step forward, hooking my right leg behind his right leg and ...

... kick back. I still push down on his shoulder ...

... and continue to do so until he hits the floor.

Back again in the real world, Ruth is pinned against the wall by an attacker who grabs her lapels.

Her reaction is instantaneous. She claws for his face.

Ruth reacts with an explosion of movement, throwing up her arms and kneeing him in the groin.

This time Ruth prepares to apply a leg lock like that shown on page 30.

She still uses a distraction technique such as the open hand to the chin.

She pushes hard with hand and knee throwing him backwards.

HELD BY THE LAPELS

Ruth is once again held against the wall by the lapels. This time she trips him using the trip shown in more detail on page 33.

Hooking her leg inside his she drives forward, lifting his leg upwards until ...

... she topples him.

Confrontation.

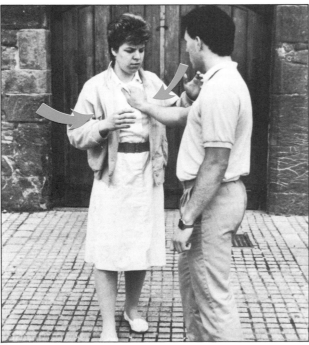

He grabs. Ruth does not draw away — she wants to keep his hand where it is.

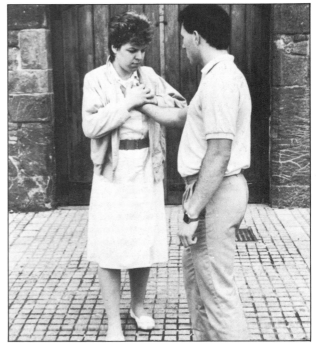

She firmly secures his hand where he has put it — as she did in the technique used in defence against hair pulls on page 62.

HELD BY THE LAPELS

She levers her hand into his wrist joint ...

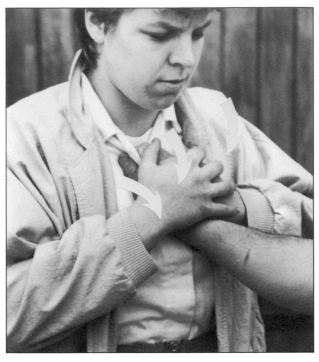

... at the same time bending forward. This cutting effect with the side of her hands, coupled to her forward body motion, causes severe pain to his wrist, enough to give **Ruth** the chance either to get away or ...

... follow with another move. In this instance she cracks her right elbow into his jaw.

Another way to release the attacker's grip on her clothing ...

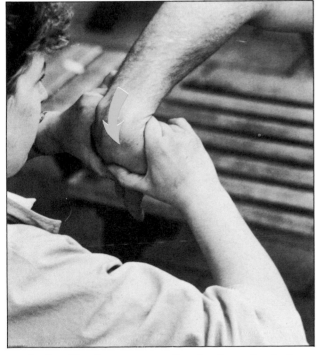

... is for Ruth to press both thumbs into the back of his hand, turning it inwards towards him.

She could then give him a nasty kick. A kick is not a token action — it must be forceful.

The attack begins. This is an all too familiar situation.

I aim both my hands at the aggressor's face. Even if I have not hit him I have distracted him.

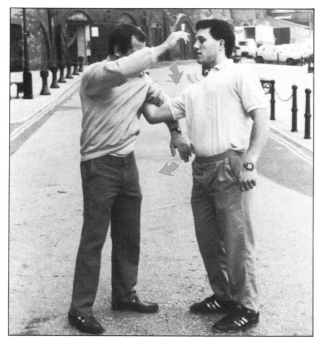

I wrap my left arm around his right arm just above the elbow joint.

I have brought my wrist up under his elbow.

This produces a painful elbow and shoulder lock.

I can now pull him to the ground and...

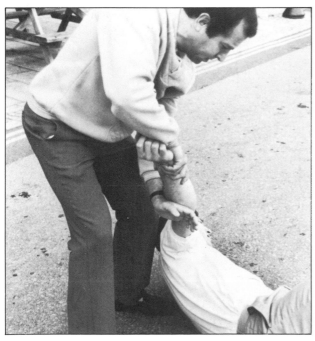

...he is open to further treatment.

Using my knee as a brace, I have his arm at snapping point.

Being held by the neck is one of the threats against which you may have to defend yourself.

Even a stranglehold lends itself to the application of now familiar techniques.

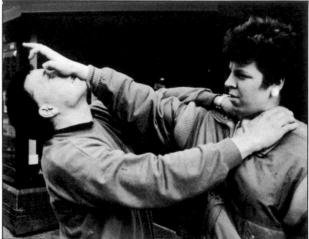

Palm to the nose with clawing fingers ...

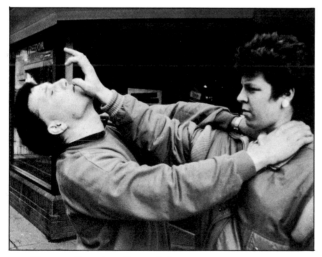

... the palm to the chin ...

... the sharp kick to the shin ...

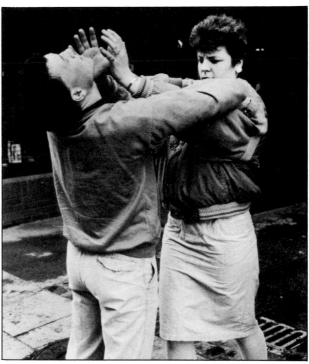

... the explosive throwing up of the arms to release the grip ...

... any strong action, the choice is yours.

Remember the distraction technique of slamming an attacker's elbow joints together?

Whatever you do make it instantaneous.
Ruth is driven back.

She rebounds ...

... and jabs her fingers into her attacker's face.

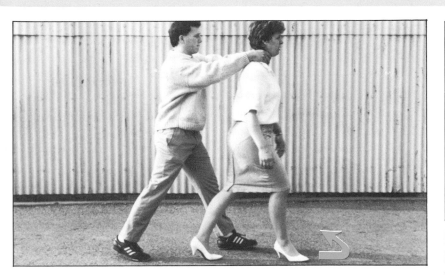

The answer to a stranglehold is movement. An attacker finds it difficult to maintain even a very firm grip if you refuse to remain in one place. If you merely move forward he will follow, always trying to maintain or increase his grip.

Ruth is gripped from behind. She does not freeze. She keeps moving forward...

... and suddenly ducks and turns under. The shoulders and neck are immensely strong and are more than a match for her aggressor's hand grip.

She comes up again. His grip is broken. You can see what a mess he's in.

Ruth can now either trip him or …

… knee him in the groin.

Ruth could have simply driven her heel back into his shin.

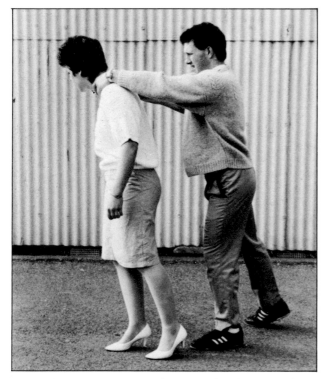

This time when she is attacked …

… Ruth swings round and drives her fist into his groin.

Even if she is attacked from the front the would-be victim can apply the technique we have just described. Continuous movement is vital.

She pulls back...

...ducks under his arm.

As she comes up (his arms have become twisted) she gives him a hefty push in the chest or by his elbows.

Here, as her attacker takes hold, Ruth's arm goes up ...

... and over. Her arm is now powerfully positioned for a backward drive ...

... into his face.

This time as soon as her attacker takes hold of her, **Ruth** strikes to his jaw.

She steps forward, slipping her right leg behind his.

She continues to push, pulling down on his sleeve. He trips over her leg and ...

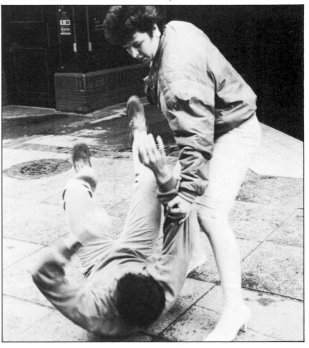

... she carries on this movement until he hits the ground.

Chris is taken by the neck. She turns her head into the crook of her attacker's elbow. This takes the pressure off her throat. She grabs his little finger and ...

... wrenches it backwards.

Again in a headlock Chris extends her arms outwards and ...

... slams them into his groin.

This time from a stranglehold from behind.

Chris thrusts back her hips and ...

... stepping forward swings her fist into his groin.

Two ways in which you may find yourself on the ground: either you are forced down or you are attacked while you are already on the ground – at a picnic or sunbathing. You are certainly in a more difficult situation in this position. The last thing you want is to end up struggling on the ground with an assailant. You must make your moves explosive and decisive – always with the object of ending up on your feet and getting away.

Harassment in the park. He closes in threateningly. Ruth catches hold of his trouser leg.

Using her legs as a ready weapon . . .

... she strikes, making good use of the heels of her shoes. This is a push and pull operation – pushing with her legs and pulling hard on his trousers.

As he is jolted backwards, she pulls hard on his leg.

She would now be wise to run.

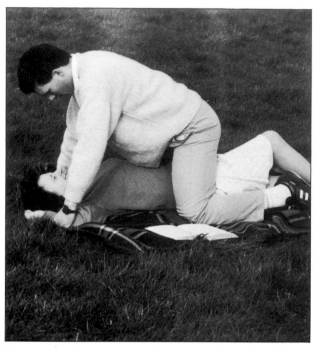

Suppose, however, the attacker pins his would-be victim to the ground.

Chris smacks her right thigh back into his buttocks, shooting him forward.

She heaves her body to the left and ...

... grabs his testicles.

Don't be squeamish! You do whatever is necessary to stop the attack. Your sole object is to disable your attacker or get away.

Another way is to bring both knees up, preparing for the explosion to follow.

As she arches and twists to her left, she claws his face. Remember, a woman defending herself has to use every means to hand.

She follows through this movement until he is thrown and she can get away.

Unwelcome attentions on the sand.

He stands over her. She already has her actions mapped out in her own mind.

In an instant she has spread-eagled her legs, forcing his wide apart.

The way is clear for a kick to the groin.

Another way: Chris crooks her left foot behind his right ankle. She raises her right leg and ...

... cracks hard into his shin. This is a leg lock as was shown on page 30.

All these techniques have one object — to gain time for an escape. Anyone in agony from a well-placed kick is unlikely to chase you.

We go back to the studio to demonstrate basic ways of avoiding a punch and turning the tables on an aggressor. You can call these "counter moves" – some of them will by now be familiar to you. The lessons to note are that you deflect the punch or move out of its way rather than get involved in a fist fight. Cowering away from the punch will not solve your problems. What you must aim to do is to take advantage of this form of attack and apply skills which I will demonstrate in the following pages.

First avoiding the punch:

You can go inside his arm.

You can go outside his arm.

Practise these movements. While you should be skilled at both these movements you may decide that the best method is to deflect his punch with an outside-the-arm move. This is because the inside-the-arm technique still leaves you in a face-to-face confrontation, whereas by deflecting his arm outside, you are no longer in the "direct line of fire". The follow-on from the deflection of a punch must be so prompt that it is essentially part of the same movement. While you can learn "moves", the lesson throughout this book is that such moves are not ends in themselves. They are always part of a more extended series of movements.

Nigel throws a punch.

I have stepped forward and deflected his arm from outside.

I grab his arm and kick his leg.

I can then follow up with a familiar strike to his arm.

This time, as I avoid Nigel's punch, I deflect with my left arm. I am again outside his arm. It is important that you practise the deflecting movement with both arms, inside and out.

I follow up with a punch to his body.

I now move inside his arm to deflect his punch ...

... and at the same time strike his face with my open palm or else I could punch or kick.

Here again, as Nigel throws a punch ...

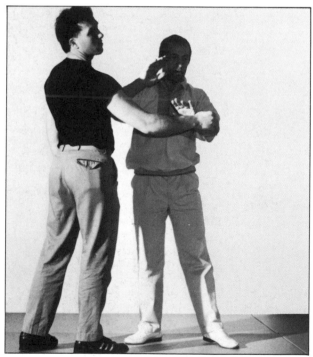

... I move inside his arm. My left arm deflects, the right arm prepares for the next move, swinging through ready to ...

... go into reverse and violently contact his chin.

When Nigel attacks, this time I respond with an arm lock. I deflect and ...

... hold his wrist. My left hand is behind his elbow joint.

A rotating movement ends like this.

I then pull with my right arm and push with my left. His arm is now in a painful lock.

I'm not finished with him yet. I push him closer to the ground with my knee. This should be enough but ...

... having brought him to the ground...

... I decide to keep him there in this hold.

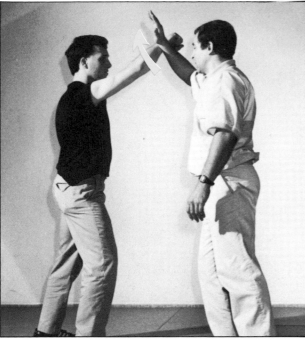

Deflecting from outside Nigel's arm, I take hold of his wrist and ...

... pull his arm down and around ...

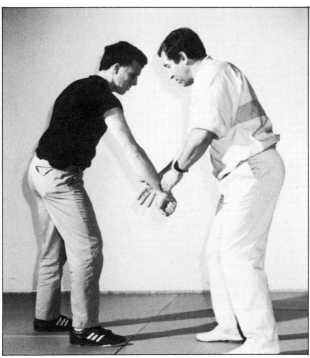

... towards my left hand.

I now change hands, grasping his arm with my left hand.

DEFENCE FROM A PUNCH

My free right arm clasps his elbow joint and with this lock ...

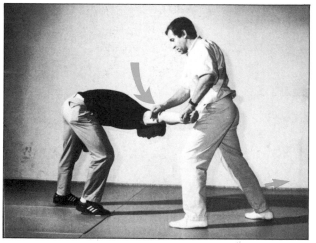

... I pull him down, at the same time stepping backwards.

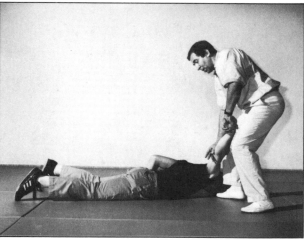

He is floored.

From this deflecting movement I shall put on a wrist lock.

I take his hand with my thumb to the back.

Then with both hands I twist his arm until he is forced to the ground.

Note that I have turned my body to the right during this action. This movement has added to the force behind the twisting of his wrist and arm.

Nigel strikes with a downward blow.

I deflect with my left arm at the same time stepping in towards him.

I take hold of his wrist ...

> Note that I have deflected the blow just as his arm is about to come down. It would be difficult to deflect if his arm had come lower and was nearer to making contact. I would then have had to respond by side-stepping or by applying a different blocking movement.

... pulling it downwards. I have brought my right arm into play.

I use both my arms to complete this lock. Note that I have stepped close to him to obtain a stronger leverage.

I can now take him to the ground by placing my right leg behind his and kicking back. You saw this move in the earlier tripping section.

These are just a few of the basic ways in which you can defend yourself against a punch. Punching, a pretty ferocious form of attack, is popular with aggressors.

In the martial arts there are many different approaches to countering punches, each of which has much to offer. I have demonstrated what I consider to be the most effective method for your purpose. If you go to self defence classes you may learn many others which, with practice, could be equally valuable.

Many violent situations develop from a war of words.

As my attacker aims a blow …

… I side-step and deflect his arm.

I grab his wrist with one hand and his elbow with the other and ...

... pull him round and ...

... keep pulling until I've got him down.

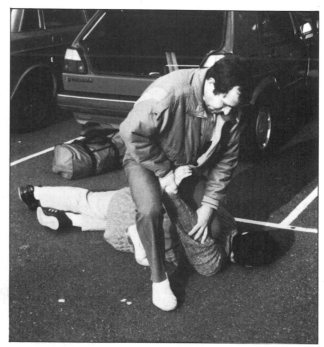

I pin him, using my knee and arm lock.

The attacker throws a punch with his left hand. I deflect it with my left hand.

I grip his wrist and, using his own movement, pull him forward. At the same time my right arm swings forward and ...

... back across his neck. This action has braced his left arm against my chest, locking his elbow joint. My right arm keeps pushing back until ...

... he's floored. Note that I still have control of his wrist.

I can now control him on the ground.

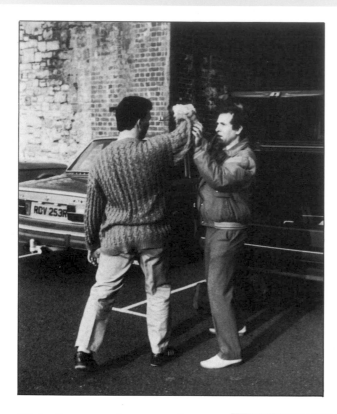

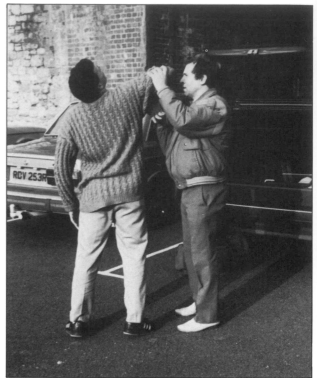

This time as the attacker aims a blow at me I take his arm into this painful lock. I am pushing up with my right hand and down with my left. This compressing action between his elbow and wrist locks the joints.

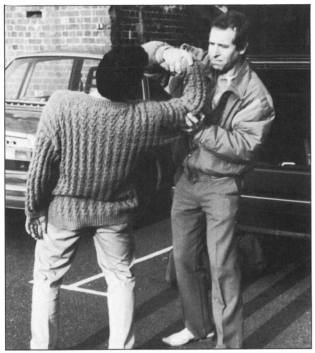

With a quick twist I bring his wrist up and his elbow down.

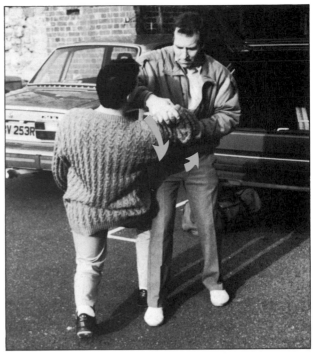

I now push his arm back and down.

He hits the floor.

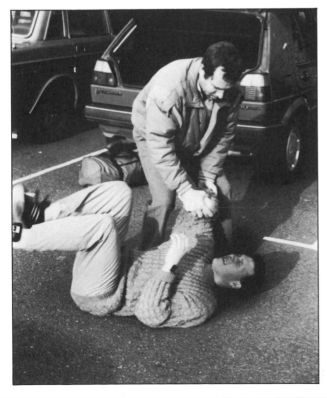

I'm ready for whatever he is about to throw at me.

He has punched. I have turned to deflect it.

I keep turning, my right arm poised for ...

... a backward blow.

In this movement I have not applied any holds but have acted with great speed. It is not a complicated technique – it just calls for practice.

Here I have deflected his blow with my left hand and struck for his face.

Having him in this weakened position I hook my left arm over his right arm and swing my body round backwards. He's in trouble. If my right arm does not hit his head ...

... it will swing backwards across his throat. My left arm is still hooked over his right arm which is braced against my back. The pressure on his elbow joint is, of course, painful.

Swinging my arm round his throat...

... forces him into a potentially back-breaking position.

The attacker is about to throw a punch.

As he steps forward I move to his side. I parry his arm with my left hand. At the same time I swing the side of my clenched fist into his groin.

Whilst he is bent forward I clutch with both hands at his collar and the back of his jacket.

I stamp on the back of his knee and ...

... he falls to the ground.

I pull back hard on his collar.

His head is forced back into a position in which I can disable him with a blow. It is important to keep your own body straight and well balanced so that you do not fall with your attacker.

Kicks can be even more vicious than punches. It is difficult to avoid a kick. If at all possible you must move quickly out of the way. However, there are certain counter-moves to a kick. As with punches you move outside or inside the aggressor's leg. Outside is usually safer.

The attack begins.

As he kicks, I step forward and outside his leg.

I turn to my left, with my left hand I scoop up his ankle.

I grip his foot in my right hand and ...

... take a big step forward, thrusting him over backwards.

This time I have come underneath his ankle with my right arm. "Any further trouble and ...

... you've had it".

I have gone inside his leg and taken control by moving in close. My right leg is poised for tripping, my right hand grasps him at the shoulder.

A push – and he's floored.

A FINAL WORD

The techniques I have demonstrated in this book can be learnt by all able-bodied people and some by the less physically robust. It is better if you take those techniques you feel most able to master and practise them constantly. This will give you the confidence and the desire to extend your *repertoire*. If you can join a self defence course with other people, I would recommend that you do so.

Everybody takes steps to protect their possessions – their car, their house. It is even more important to protect yourself. Unfortunately, with the increase in violence, it is becoming more and more necessary for the ordinary person to be prepared. Your instinct for self preservation can be reinforced by practice and training. This book should take you a considerable way along that road.

The author takes a self defence class with a group of young adults from the Royal School for the Deaf, Exeter.

ACKNOWLEDGEMENTS

I acknowledge with thanks the enthusiastic and skilful help I have had in getting this book together from my student and friend Nigel Hoskins, my elder daughter Ruth, both black belts; and my wife Chris who has always been a vital part of our martial arts world. My close friend Stan Griffiths, veteran and master of the martial arts, has been a constant inspiration and source of encouragement. I am also grateful to the Devon and Cornwall Constabulary, Middlemoor, Exeter, for their generosity with information and advice. My sessions with Women's Institute groups have always been productive of ideas, many of which have been useful in the writing of this book. My mother and father Mabel and Harold Goldman have also helped in many practical ways.

USEFUL ADDRESSES

UNIVERSAL BUDO ASSOCIATION

Secretary
21 St John's Road
Withycombe
Exmouth
Devon EX8 4BY
Tel (0395) 265532

AMATEUR MARTIAL ASSOCIATION

120 Cromer Street
London WC1H 8BS
Tel 01 837 4406

SPORTS COUNCIL

16 Upper Woburn Place
London WC1H 0QP
Tel 01 388 1277

CARDIFF SCHOOL OF BUDO

Fairoak Hall
Fairoak Road
Cardiff CF2 4PX

YOUR LOCAL LIBRARY

YOUR LOCAL SPORTS CENTRE